21st Century Junior Library

MAKING A DIFFERENCE WITH THE HUMANE SOCIETY

Katie Marsico

How Can I Help?

Published in the United States of America by:

CHERRY LAKE PRESS
2395 South Huron Parkway, Suite 200, Ann Arbor, MI 48104
www.cherrylakepress.com

Reading Adviser: Marla Conn, Read With Me Now
Photo Credits: © FatCamera/iStock.com, cover, title page; © Clbnkbb/Dreamstime.com, 5; © Andrii Zastrozhnov/Dreamstime.com, 6; © MB SS08-42/Shutterstock, 7; © Heritage Image Partnership Ltd/Alamy Stock Photo, 9; © Bigandt/Dreamstime.com, 10; Library of Congress, National Photo Company Collection, 12; © John Salangsang/Invision for The Humane Society of the United States/AP Images, 13; © hedgehog94/Shutterstock, 14; © Christopher Berkey/ASSOCIATED PRESS, 17; © Sirinarth Mekvorawuth/Dreamstime.com, 18; © Caroline Klapper/Dreamstime.com, 19; © Alex Gulevich/Dreamstime.com, 20; © David P Baileys/Shutterstock, 21

Cherry Lake Press is an imprint of Cherry Lake Publishing Group.

Library of Congress Cataloging-in-Publication Data

Names: Marsico, Katie, 1980- author.
Title: Making a difference with the humane society / by Katie Marsico.
Description: Ann Arbor, MI : Cherry Lake Publishing, [2024] | Series: How can I help? | Audience: Grades 2-3 | Summary: "The Humane Society asks each of us to be a hero for all animals. Readers will explore the history and impact of this organization and how staff and volunteers work tirelessly to ensure no animals are left suffering in our communities"– Provided by publisher.
Identifiers: LCCN 2024010013 | ISBN 9781668946817 (hardcover) | ISBN 9781668948200 (paperback) | ISBN 9781668949726 (ebook) | ISBN 9781668954287 (pdf)
Subjects: LCSH: Humane Society of the United States–History–Juvenile literature. | Animal welfare–United States–Juvenile literature.
Classification: LCC HV4763.H8524 M37 2024 | DDC 179/.3/06073–dc23/eng/20240311
LC record available at https://lccn.loc.gov/2024010013

Cherry Lake Publishing Group would like to acknowledge the work of the Partnership for 21st Century Learning, a Network of Battelle for Kids. Please visit Battelle for Kids online for more information.

Printed in the United States of America

CHERRY LAKE PRESS

CONTENTS

COMBATING CRUELTY

Many pets live with people who love and care for them. Sadly, this is not the case for all animals. In the United States and Canada alone, millions of dogs and cats are without homes. Others experience **neglect** or **abuse**.

Humane societies help these creatures. A humane society is a **nonprofit** organization that helps protect animals.

Animals need many of the same things we do to survive.

Think!

Think about the different roles that animals play in humans' lives. Now think about some of the challenges that animals face. Why do you think it's important for people to take steps to protect them?

Humane societies are found all over the world. They include the Humane Society of the United States (HSUS) and the Canadian Federation of Humane Societies (CFHS). These groups try to ensure that animals are treated with respect and **compassion**.

Humane societies are overwhelmed by unwanted kittens each year.

The HSUS and CFHS help pets. They also help animals involved in scientific research, farming, and entertainment.

A HISTORY OF HUMANE SOCIETIES

The first humane society was formed in London, England, in 1824. It was called the Royal Society for the Prevention of Cruelty to Animals. Its members were concerned with improving the **welfare** of the pit pony, a small horse that helped in coal mines. Pit ponies were often overworked, underfed, and abused.

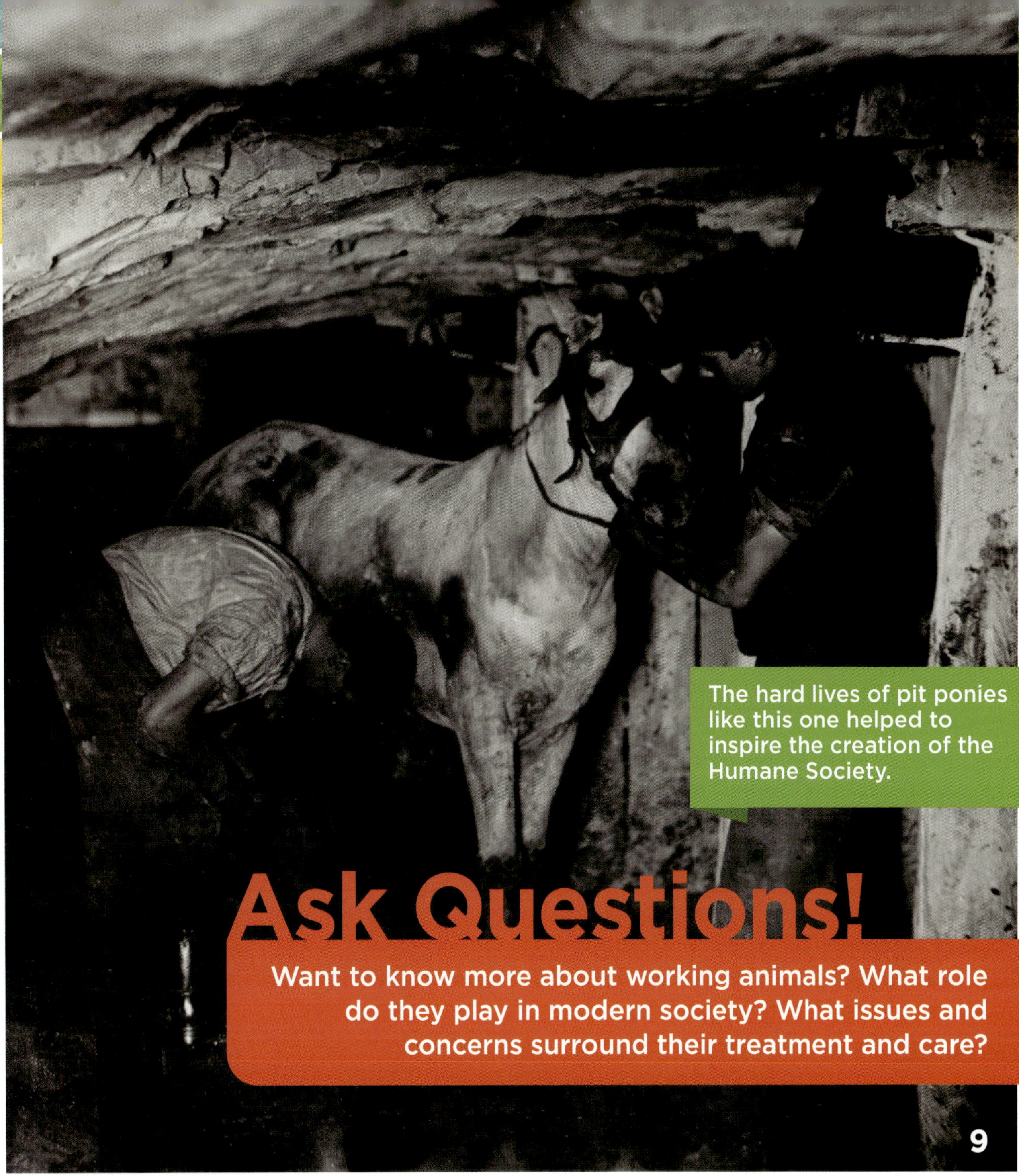

The hard lives of pit ponies like this one helped to inspire the creation of the Humane Society.

Ask Questions!

Want to know more about working animals? What role do they play in modern society? What issues and concerns surround their treatment and care?

Members of London's humane society raised public awareness about the cruelty that pit ponies experienced. They also succeeded in creating laws to protect working animals.

Animals do a lot of work for humans. Humane societies make sure these animals are well cared for.

Think!

Think about the work that animal shelters and rescues do. Many run adoption programs to help unwanted pets find new homes. Why do you think humane societies encourage people to adopt an animal instead of buying one from a pet store?

Eventually, people began forming humane societies outside of England. These groups focused on several different animal welfare issues. In some cases, members **lobbied** for better treatment of farm animals. In others, they built shelters for **strays** and unwanted pets.

U.S. citizens formed the HSUS in 1954. Three years later, residents of Canada founded the CFHS. These organizations helped unite smaller, local animal-welfare groups throughout the two countries that had been operating since the 1860s. They made it easier to address animal-welfare issues at a national level.

Small animal rescue organizations like this one were the foundation for the Humane Societies in the United States and Canada.

Make a Guess!

Can you guess where the HSUS and CFHS get the money they need to operate? Did you say that most of their funding comes from membership dues and donations? If you did, you'd be right!

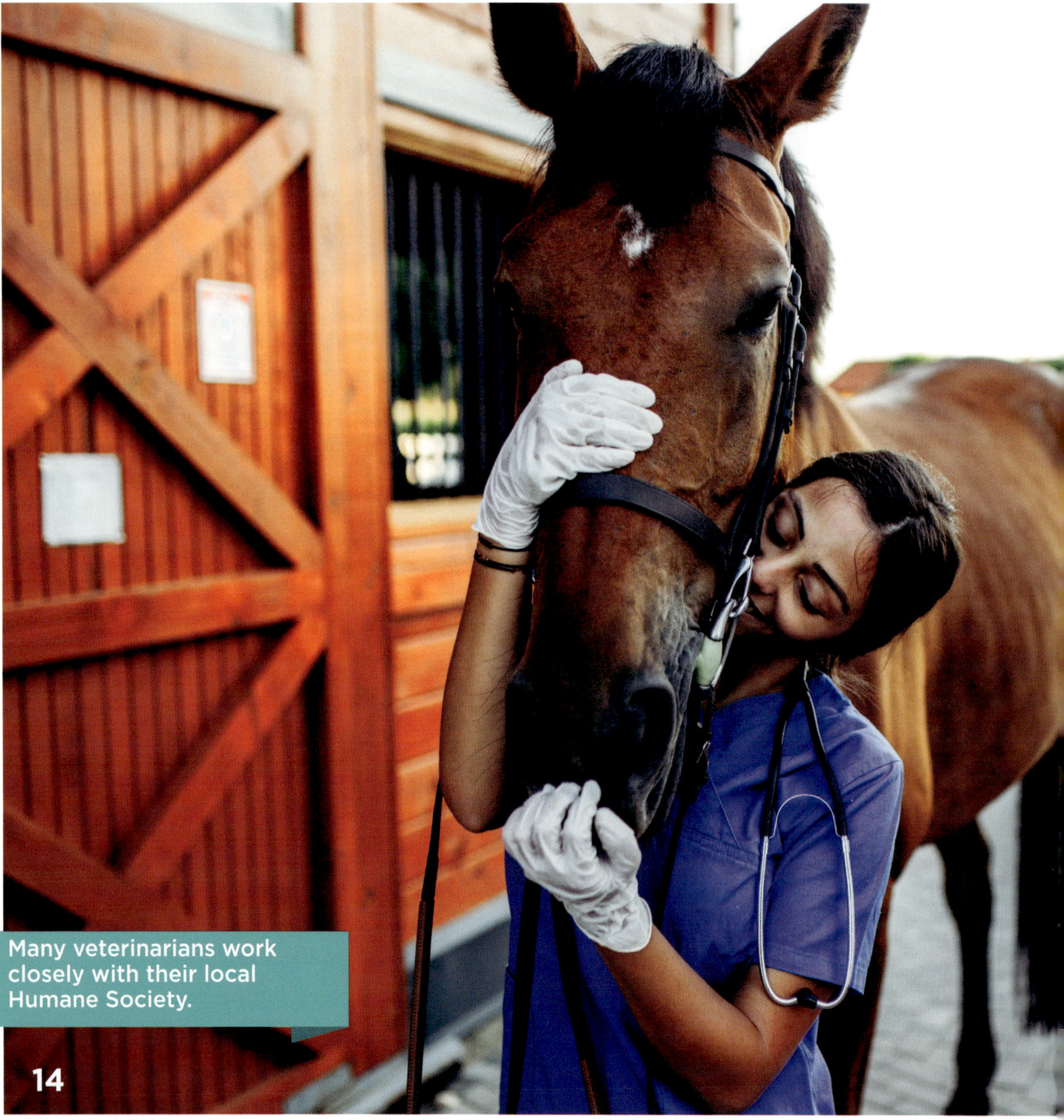

Many veterinarians work closely with their local Humane Society.

Ask Questions!

Want to know more about what it takes to work with the HSUS or CFHS? Write, e-mail, or call either organization to find out!

Today, the HSUS and CFHS depend on several types of workers to protect animals. These include veterinarians, **biologists**, and experts in animal behavior. Lawyers and criminal investigators are other examples of humane society employees. Volunteers also donate their time and effort to help the organizations prevent animal suffering.

CREATING A KINDER WORLD

The HSUS and CFHS support the humane treatment of animals. They often carry out investigations. They observe how animals are being cared for in a variety of settings. These range from circuses and laboratories to farms and people's homes. They also pay close attention to threats that wild animals face, including illegal hunting.

This elephant sanctuary in Tennessee cares for retired and rescued circus and zoo elephants.

Make a Guess!

Can you guess how many animals are assisted by organizations such as the HSUS? Think big! The HSUS reports that it helps provide lifesaving support to 440,000 animals.

All animals should be treated fairly—this includes animals on farms, in circuses and movies, and in your own neighborhood.

If the HSUS and CFHS find that abuse or neglect is occurring, they sometimes conduct rescue operations. They help suffering animals receive medical care and shelter.

The HSUS and CFHS also work closely with government officials. They try to create laws that prevent animal cruelty from occurring in the first place.

Look!

Head online with an adult. Look for information about what the HSUS, CFHS, or another humane society is doing in your area. Can you find photos of these groups helping to prevent local animal cruelty?

Finally, a large part of what the two organizations do involves education. They offer training programs for animal-welfare groups that teach workers how to assist animals in need.

Caring for neglected and injured animals is an important job.

Create!

Are you interested in supporting the HSUS and CFHS? Grab some crayons, markers, and poster board. Create posters explaining animal-welfare issues that these groups are trying to address. Ask if you can hang them around your community!

The HSUS and CFHS also organize media campaigns to raise public awareness about animal-welfare issues. This helps shape a more humane world. Since animals cannot speak for themselves, it is up to humans to speak up for them.

GLOSSARY

abuse **(ah-BYOOS)** improper treatment

biologists **(bye-AH-luh-jists)** scientists who study living things, including plants and animals

compassion **(kuhm-PAA-shuhn)** pity and concern for the suffering of others

humane **(hyoo-MAYN)** demonstrating compassion

lobbied **(LAH-beed)** sought to influence lawmakers or public officials on a particular issue

neglect **(nih-GLEKT)** the state of being uncared for

nonprofit **(nahn-PRAH-fit)** not existing for the main purpose of earning more money than is spent

strays **(STRAYZ)** animals such as cats and dogs that have no home

welfare **(WEL-fair)** the happiness, health, and well-being of an individual or group

FIND OUT MORE

Books

Clendening, John. *Animal Shelters*. New York: PowerKids Press, 2015.

Markovics, Joyce. *Dogs*. Ann Arbor, MI: Cherry Lake Press, 2024.

Markovics, Joyce. *Courageous Cats*. Ann Arbor, MI: Cherry Lake Press, 2025.

Websites

With an adult, find out more online with these suggested searches.

Canadian Federation of Humane Societies—Hey Kids!
Head here to learn more about preventing animal cruelty.

The Humane Society of the United States—Just for Kids
Read articles about animal welfare and to learn more about supporting the HSUS.

INDEX

ABOUT THE AUTHOR

Katie Marsico is the author of more than 200 children's books. She lives in a suburb of Chicago, Illinois, with her husband and children.